JOETRY

JOETRY

Well-Selected Lyrix from Six Decades . . . of Song

Mendelson Joe

ECW

Published by ECW Press
665 Gerrard Street East
Toronto, Ontario, Canada M4M 1Y2
416-694-3348 / info@ecwpress.com

Cover images by Mendelson Joe

LIBRARY AND ARCHIVES CANADA CATALOGUING IN PUBLICATION

Title: Joetry : well-selected lyrix from six decades...of song / Mendelson Joe.

Names: Mendelson Joe, 1944– author.

Identifiers: Canadiana (print) 2020021392X
Canadiana (ebook) 2020021425X |

ISBN 978-1-77041-551-5 (softcover)
ISBN 978-1-77305-598-5 (PDF)
ISBN 978-1-77305-597-8 (EPUB)

Subjects: LCSH: Songs, English—Canada—Texts.

Classification: LCC ML54 .6 .M537 2020
DDC 782.42164026/8—dc23

The publication of *Joetry* has been generously supported by the Canada Council for the Arts which last year invested $153 million to bring the arts to Canadians throughout the country and is funded in part by the Government of Canada. *Nous remercions le Conseil des arts du Canada de son soutien. L'an dernier, le Conseil a investi 153 millions de dollars pour mettre de l'art dans la vie des Canadiennes et des Canadiens de tout le pays. Ce livre est financé en partie par le gouvernement du Canada.* We acknowledge the support of the Ontario Arts Council (OAC), an agency of the Government of Ontario, which last year funded 1,737 individual artists and 1,095 organizations in 223 communities across Ontario for a total of $52.1 million. We also acknowledge the contribution of the Government of Ontario through the Ontario Book Publishing Tax Credit, and through Ontario Creates for the marketing of this book.

ONTARIO CREATES

ONTARIO ARTS COUNCIL
CONSEIL DES ARTS DE L'ONTARIO
an Ontario government agency
un organisme du gouvernement de l'Ontario

Canada Council for the Arts
Conseil des Arts du Canada
Canada

PRINTED AND BOUND IN CANADA

PRINTING: COPYWELL 5 4 3 2 1

In memory of Daryl Leberg

Contents

Foreword

In the early eighties, when I was a singer-songwriter working in Toronto, Mendelson Joe called me early one morning, introduced himself and asked if I would sing on a recording. Although I hadn't met him, I knew of his reputation as a painter and performer, songwriter and musician, and we had many friends in common. On the phone his manner was abrupt, and I felt unnerved. Still, I said yes because I admired him, I love to sing, and I was curious. In person, I thought he suited his voice. He is a large man with a straightforward demeanor. In the studio, he gave me no direction other than to sing what felt right. On that session with him, and those that followed, I had the time of my life. I felt I could do no wrong, an unusual sensation when recording. He trusted me and respected what I delivered.

As I have since learned, when M. Joe believes in your work as a songwriter, poet, singer, novelist, composer, visual artist, musician, activist, or visionary, you will know it — unqualifiedly. He is unafraid to express his appreciation and, often joyously, declare he has been moved. He is a magnanimous man.

The vibrancy that lives in the man is transmitted through every brush stroke, guitar chord, lyric, and poem. He is a repository of creative impulse, and the different mediums he works in serve to flesh out the total artist called Mendelson Joe.

Letter writing is not a forgotten art for Joe. He's a ferocious correspondent who doesn't do email. I am likely only one of many people with a huge file of saved letters and postcards from him. Themselves works of art, colourful missives, mine are addressed to Madam Artist, Madam Genius, and — once — to Madam Obliqueness from M Obtuse. National papers frequently publish his letters.

Joetry is a collection of poems that live a parallel life as Mendelson Joe song lyrics. The words are shining gems in both settings, but here, exposed on the page, the pithy insights and vivid pictures come to the foreground.

It's easy to dive in, easy to be seduced by poems that cuddle and snuggle. Mendelson Joe calls himself a fragile man, and he doesn't shy away from tenderness. He has a special regard for women and the power of women. His love poems make clear that he loves women, men, bears, action, art, friendship . . . he loves love.

Joe confronts sexism, apathy, greed, power imbalance, cruelty, destruction of the environment — and stresses his conviction that we are running out of time. He's frustrated and anxious, and he radiates urgency. He wants all of us to wake up.

He, himself, does not escape his own notice. Self-descriptions range from the king of humility to a big old baby to a cockroach.

Still, he never stops examining his actions and never stops trying to put things right.

Worlds collide on this bumpy road. You can be taken by surprise with notions like waterskiing on swan lake, and gripped by direct language that doesn't exclude the unusual. I note words like "pulchritude" and "prorogation." Not common poetry parlance.

Fearless and direct, tender and loving — the marriage of these forces is electric. In *Joetry*, Mendelson Joe fixes his gaze on the beauty in people, nature, work, love, deeds, words, and accountability — the often unheralded, everyday stuff of life. He is casting a wide net, trying to reach us all, telling us clearly: appreciate what is good and beautiful, do the right things, stop doing the wrong things, laugh, create, speak up, sing, love, and respect the earth and one another. Oh, one more thing: revere women — they are our best hope for the future of life on the planet.

Mendelson Joe says it's his fate to write, paint, sing, play guitar, write letters. He's prolific and unstoppable, the canary in our coal mine. I find his world irresistible and the publication of *Joetry* timely. For fifty years, Joe has prodded and charmed, exhorting us to press for better human behaviour and to appreciate love in every form. Now, as it was from early on, I am a willing follower. When I read *Joetry*, I feel alive. When he says to "dance with Joe / don't be a schmoe," I'm there on the dance floor with him.

Gwen Swick
Elora, Ontario

Alien

I knew a rare lady
She was the mother of four
She was fired by the Colonel
For watching a sunset
She was an alien

Then I knew a rare man
Who wrote from his heart
And he looked for a door
He sang on his toes
He was an alien

It's the same old story
It's the same old song
It makes no damn difference
Because they don't belong
They are aliens

I once lived with an angel
And she cried for the planet
Then she went off to France
Just to pull down her pants
She was an alien

Read Nadia Halim's biography of this Joe alien (*ALIEN* is available through ECW Press).

All Things Living

Genuine
I mean Jennifleur
She says it's all just molecules
Moving molecules
Beyond the beyond
In perpetuity
Perpetuity
All things living

Then there was
Linginee
He stood for nothing
He settled for anything
That's where the money was
All things living
We are

The sun she keeps a-sunning
The moon she keeps a-mooning
The Joes they keep a-Joeing
The snows they keep a-snowing
The Smoo's they keep a-Smooing
We are

Annie Smith

I was painting a painting
Singing a song
Doing my job

A letter arrived
It was not contrived
From a female fan

Her name was Smith,
Annie Smith
And she spoke her mind

So I wrote her a postcard
And stamped it real hard
And I mailed it quick

Annie Smith,
She is not a myth
She's a large child

The day we met
I sang a set
And a song for her
Then we dined
It was summertime

She alleged we met in The Riverboat on Yorkville Avenue in the 70's. I question that fact.

Then we talked
And we ran

Annie Smith,
She is not a myth
She's a large child

The colours fell
Now there's snow on the tennis court
She paints her paintings,
Dances her dance
And snores her snore

Annie Smith,
She is not a myth
She's a large child

Born to Cuddle

I was born in July
Nineteen forty-four
Millions did perish
But not little me
I was born free
I was born to cuddle
I was born

Twenty years later
Nineteen sixty-four
I took to the stage
Out of my cage
Still little me
I was born free
I was born to cuddle
I was born

I was born to cuddle
Like a fat furry animal
Put on this planet
To put something back

I was born to cuddle

Twenty years after
Nineteen eighty-four
George Orwell's prediction
It came true
And so much more
Still little me
I was born free
I was born to cuddle
I was born

Cold Old

I am cold, I am old
But I have warm thoughts
Of a world
Of a time
When lies are obsolete

I am cold, I am old
But I've got experience
To be strong
When I'm wrong
We all must face this music

I am cold, I am old
But I've got conscience
I have ruth
I seek truth
We all must face this music

It's all music to my eyes
Music to my heart
It's all music
Music to my brain
I am sane

I was literally cold
this morning and I'm
literally old.

I am cold and I am old
But I have a big chest
That I beat
I repeat
We all must face this music

I am cold and I am old
And I wear bunny ears
Every day is Halloween
Focus on the dream
Am I communicating?

Denise

She's blonde and affectionate
And anyone's friend
Feed her and love her
She'll be yours to the end

Her eyes are brown
As the earth oh so sad
Indulge her with treats and caresses

But leave her alone
When you're not at home
She'll go for the garbage
Like a doggy

Gold as the barley
Of Saskatchewan
She's eager to please
Like a talk-show host

But leave her alone
When you're not at home
She'll go for the garbage
Like a doggy

I'm an animal rights
advocate, especially bears.

Everybody Talks

I play the music
And the music plays me
When everybody talks
And nobody seems to care

My name is Joe
I come from To-ron-ron-to
Where everybody talks
And nobody seems to care

Everybody talks
And nobody seems to care
Who does what
And what to whom
It ain't fair

See you later alligator
In a while crocodile
When everybody talks
And nobody seems to care

Everbody talks
And nobody seems to care
Who does what
And what to whom
It ain't fair

I wrote this one back in the 80's when I was playing in the basement vomitorium of the Colonial Tavern on Yonge Street in Toronto.

Game of Love

Deal me in when you play
That game called love
Deal me in for mortal sin
The game is blind
But I don't mind

Deal me in when you play
That game called love

The stakes are high
When you play that game called love
The stakes are high
And so am I

Deal me in when you play
That game called love

Jack's are wild
When you play that game called love
This Jack is wild
Just to be your child
The cards are hot
For what you've got

Deal me in when you play
That game called love

I'm not much of a game player.

Misanthropic Man

I am a misanthropic man
And I love to dance
But not in France
I don't hate the French
Nor do I hate the Germans
But they left their mark
No pun intended
Fun intended
Fun intended
Fun

I love to dance
But not in Chile
Except by invitation to
Pinochet's funeral
I love to dance
And move my body
Like Michael Jackson

I love to dance
But I do not cha cha
Do not mambo
Do not tango
But I like Tchaikovsky
What about Mendelson?
Fun intended

I have problems with humans, especially hypocrites.

No Trespassing

No trespassing here
Honey, I don't want you around
Because I am spoke for
I am loved
By some other lady

I said
No trespassing here
Honey, I don't want you around
I am mindful
And you caused me
Much pain
And I know it
No trespassing here
I am normal
And I am easily seducted
And you know it
No trespassing here

Being famous is a medical problem.

The Name of the Game Ain't Schmaltz

Patience is a virtue
I don't know
Greed is the seed
It's a sickness
Of most men's souls
But the name of my game
It's always the same
The name of the game ain't schmaltz
It's results

Talk is sweet
But it sure doesn't pay my rent
Survivin' your jivin'
When all my money
Is spent

The name of this man's game
Is always the same
The name of the game ain't schmaltz
It's results

A.P.A.

I woke up this morning
It was just passed noon
I turned on the TV
And drank five beers
Then I got into my Audi
And drove to the Loblaws
To buy some smokes
And told some jokes
About the Niggers and Jews

I got the A.P.A., I got the A.P.A.
I got the T.H.Y.
You say why?
Because I am ignorant
That's me

Then I drove back home
And beat up on the wife
And watched TV
And drank three beers
Then I drank three more
Then I drove downtown
To hear some rock and roll
I like the Rolling Stones
They satisfy my soul

I got the A.P.A., I got the A.P.A.
I got the T.H.Y.
You say why?
Because I'm ignorant
That's me

Then I got real stupid
And got real drunk
Me and all my good friends
We played backgammon
Then we scored some drugs
And we got real high
Me and all my good friends
We played backgammon
Then we watched P.T.L.
I got the A.P.A., I got the A.P.A.
I got the T.H.Y.
You say why?
Because I'm ignorant
That's me

Art Is the healer

Let it be said, I am a man of science. As a man of science my time is short but I've lived long and I've lived true to what I know and hope to learn because art is the healer, it's what I know, so I say . . . sing of crayons, I say sing of saxophones, sing of possibility, sing of poetry. Cremate me crispy but DANCE WITH JOE and wear a helmet. It's what I know. Thank you.

*

Canuckian

I've been to heaven, it was before I was seven
Maybe I was five, maybe I was four
And I've been to Hope and there I learned to cope
And play guitar — I'm learning so far

Because I am Canuckian, Canucky, Lucky, Duckian
I've been to Ignace, Atikokan and Guelph
and Saskatoon, I sang that Saska-tune
And then I played Port Dover, Rush and I went over
And then Sault Ste. Marie, I was still married to Flea
Because she was Canuckian

I am Canuckian

I've been to Sudbury and played Calgary
I met Dodi from Didsbury, she was kind to me
That was '64 long, long before Jim Keegstra taught history
He was home on the range
That was long ago, I was just nine and teen
You know what I mean

I am Canuckian

Canary in the Coalmine

I don't know where to go
To sing my song when no one listens
When no one listens, no one listens
It is my job, it is my truth
The words are sad, they are not couth

Canary in the coalmine I am
Canary in the coalmine I am

Human beans, it's Man I mean
He's very stupid
He fouls his nest
Then he fouls his nest
And then he rapes his children
And then he rapes their future
And all things living, this is the song

Canary in the coalmine I am
Canary in the coalmine I am

Melody is not the key to this song
It is the words
Hear me now before I croak
You'll be next
It is no joke

Canary in the coalmine I am
Canary in the coalmine I am

Dance with Joe

Come on baby, don't say maybe
We're gonna eat pizza
And dance to Tchaikovsky

Dance with Joe
Don't be a schmoe
Dance toe to toe
Come on and dance with Joe

You be the swan
And I'll be the prince
We'll fall in love
Dancing to Swan Lake

Dance with Joe
Don't be a schmoe
Dance toe to toe
Come on and dance with Joe

There are no water skiers
On Swan Lake
Just romance
May I have this dance?

Dance with Joe
Don't be a schmoe
Dance toe to toe
Come on and dance with Joe

Dreamin'

When I think of you
I close my eyes I do
I'm dreamin' of you

When your eyes they meet mine
The feeling is sublime
I'm dreamin', I'm dreamin' of you

Your voice is choice
My fantasies rejoice
When I'm dreamin'
Dreamin' of you

Your wit is so true
For me it is the glue
When I'm dreamin'
I'm dreamin' of you

Excuse Me

Excuse me for interrupting
Your perversion, your feculence
But have you considered an alternative
For impotence as a way of living

Excuse me for bursting that balloon
That you inhabit
And the security and the mediocrity
All consolations for self-betrayal

Excuse me but how did you lose?
Was it in a convenience store?
Or just in passing?
By a yield sign
By the roadside of life
En route to Deadsville

Excuse me or,
Better, use me
This poet is writing and it's so exciting
To be angry, to be smitten
By the bug of balladry
So please excuse me, excuse me, excuse me

Fragile Man

I'm a fragile man
I'm in a fragile world
Near the end of time
That's if you're watching the clock

I don't mean to be
confrontational
But it's time to face
this music

You can take a stand
Or take a fall
You can demonstrate
Or give it all

Or give to no one
You can lick the bag
Of submission
Like lambs to the slaughter

Make new mistakes
Make new mistakes

Get Down To

I've got to get down to the reasons why
The world is blind so unkind to you
I've got to get down to the rights and the wrongs
The world is blind so unkind to you
I've got to get down to when it's time to move on home
The world is blind so unkind to you

Growing Pain

I've got growing pain
And it ain't the same
As the measles
My foot won't stop shaking
My belly won't stop aching
I ain't teasing you

I say please get right over
I won't take no for an answer
Can't you see
You have misjudged me
Can't you tell
That I ain't feelin' that well

Hot Meal

Sitting in the backyard
Painting three paintings
You are writing your writings
On childhood behaviour

Blossoms on the fruit trees
Everywhere greenery
Even goldfish scenery
And you say:

How 'bout a hot meal
You say how 'bout a hotmeal
Hot meal mmm, hot meal mmm
Everyone likes a hotmeal

There is redding on my big arms
Just to cradle your aggressiveness
And to savour your pulchritude
And the meaning of life, yes the meaning of life
And you say:

How 'bout a hot meal
You say how 'bout a hotmeal
Hot meal mmm, hot meal mmm
Everyone likes a hotmeal

Yes the meaning of life
It’s so fundamental
Like nipple in the mouth
Like nipple in the mouth
And you say:

How ’bout a hot meal
You say how ’bout a hotmeal
Hot meal mmm, hot meal mmm
Everyone likes a hotmeal

How Can It Be?

How can it be
After so many centuries
Of biblical teachings
We're still at war
Over whose God is best,
Whose God is best?
How can it be?

Isn't it time
We switched this rhyme
And fostered equitability
And listened to the hearts of women
Just to stop this war
Over whose God is best

Whose God is best?

There is no rest from divisiveness
There is no rest from self-appointed delusional men
Holy, holy, holy men

If I were a risk taker,
I mean a betting man
I'd bet on Rachel Carson
I'd bet on Pam Palmater

Over the likes of mercenary sycophants
They kill for a dollar
Over whose God is best

We need philosophers
We need philosophers
We need philosophers

Humans Bug Me

I was driving with a former friend
In his Porsche
They are a work of art

Then he lowered his window
And out he threw
An empty pop can
What a statement
Humans bug me

My next door neighbour
He's a liar
Pardon me,
a real estate broker

Lecher of lechers
He dyes his hair
To camouflage
His true colours

Humans bug me
Humans bug me

Macho morons
With tattoos

They walk their pitbulls
They want to be tough guys

Fouling sidewalks
But never theirs
I say leash the men
Not the doggies

Humans bug me
Humans bug me

Politicians dance
a dirty dance
of deception
I mean democracy

Of the rich
By the rich
For the rich
To keep the stupid
Stupid

Humans bug me
Humans bug me

Of all the creatures
on this earth

there's nothing,
nothing,
nothing
lower
than a human

Humans bug me
Humans bug me

I Am Normal

I was picking my nose in my Sunday clothes
Thinking 'bout my sister Sybil
Lickety-split, I almost shit, I damn near swallowed my gum

It was my good friend from way back when
We used to go to high school
A cop to me, a freak to him, I damn near swallowed my gum

I told him: I am normal!

I shook his hand and he shook mine
As I looked into his eyes
The words we spoke but missed their mark
His scope had dwindled some

I told him: I am normal!

I Think I'm Losing My Marbles

I think I'm losing my marbles
I tell you it's a doggone shame
There are so many deranged people
They are driving me to be insane

I like a little woman
Who loves me so fine
When I eat my honey
I take my time

I think I'm losing my marbles
I tell you it's a doggone shame

I think I'm losing my marbles
The doctor says I don't have too much time
I think I'm losing my marbles
You give me pills to ease my little mind

I like a little honey
I like a little cheese
Chocolate's alright
But don't you give me disease

I think I'm losing my marbles
I tell you it's a doggone shame

I Value You

Broccoli's are little trees
For my mouth and my survival
On this Earth we call our Mother
Still she turns and that I value

I value you, I value you I do
I value you, I value you it's true

Goodness me I'd love to be
free as freesia in a painting
But goodness true requires do
Action speaks, it's what I value

I value you, I value you I do
I value you, I value you it's true

Healthy minds and healthy hearts
Make for hope and generosity
Of the spirit and of the conscience
Values I cherish, values I value

I value you, I value you I do
I value you, I value you it's true

I'm a Folkie

So many times I have scratched my head
Thinking 'bout the humans, the living and the dead
And the dancing delusion, suicidal confusion
While the Big, Big Mummy sheds Big tears

I'm a folkie, ain't no jokie

Inventing our way sure ain't gonna pay
For all the harm we have done
Because the mantra is greed
The mantra is greed
While the Big, Big Mummy sheds Big tears

I'm a folkie, ain't no jokie

How many days, how many ways
Does it take to kill the Big Mummy?
Because humans are cancer
God is not the answer
He's just a placebo
Can you say placebo?

I'm a folkie, ain't no jokie

I've Been Lucky

I've been wrong
I've been right
I've been heavy
I've been light
I've been fooled
I've been fired
I've been wired
I've been tired
I've been lucky

Inside I Hide

Inside I hide
A key to words that tell
And what that all really, really means to me
It means I wish you all well
Because I want to live
And I want to give
And I give this song to you
Because that's all that I can do

Inside I hide
Fairy tales and dreams
What that all really, really means
It means I'm a child
Because I want to live
And I want to give
And I give this song to you
Because that's all that I can do

Inside I hide
"A wanting to be loved" you say
And that's how it is for me
That's how it has to be
Because I want to live
And I want to give
And I give this song to you
Because that's all that I can do

I wrote this in '73 when attending a song festival in Sopot, Poland.

It's My Fate

I've got a frustrated feeling inside me
I've got anxieties I cannot hide that you can see

Can you appreciate my fate, I know it's my fate

Every morning when I get up
I wonder when will they stop

Can you appreciate my fate, I know it's my fate

The doctor says "you are hyper"
I answer you are correct in your diagnosis doctor sir

Can you appreciate my fate, I know it's my fate

Just To Lie With You

She brings me her poems
Or prose to be true
And bread that is moist
And ham sweetly smoked

A feast for my vision
All packaged in crimson
She's vital and loving
Feline be mine
Feline be mine

Just to lie with you
And breathe your fragrance
Beneath your breast
I am your baby
I am your island
I am your mentor
And you are mine

As sure as the wind blows
As sure as the snows will snow
The clock signals hugging time
The clock signals smooching time

We exit in darkness
Fresh bread in the air
We kiss by the bus stop
On different stairs

Just to lie with you
And breathe your fragrance
Beneath your breast
I am your baby
I am your island
I am your mentor
And you are mine

Lick and Sniff

I get up each morning
And I work real hard
To paint this painting
Of the way the world is

Then I write some writings
And do the Joe-jobs
To get that watercress
Then I think of you

Lick and sniff
The one you love
Like a mango
Like a mango

Then it's back to the salt mine
At least it's my mine
Just to savour this freedom
She keeps me hungry for

Lick and sniff
The one you love
Like a mango
Like a mango

Then I tune this gitar
And make some magic
Yes, she soothes like medicine
I am a doctor, I am a doctor

Lick and sniff
The one you love
Like a mango
Like a mango

Long Long Time

It's been a long long time
I've been making rhyme
About the things that I saw
And what I believe
From my little boat

It's been a long long time
That I've been keeping time
With this trusty old foot
And my sense of truth
Though it's not so couth
From my little boat

I want to tell you
That boat is mine

It's been a long long time
That I've been painting this picture
The snow is still blue
And the moon is too
From my little boat

I want to tell you
That boat is mine

Mongers of the Lie

Good morning everybody it's a new day
Blooming like a rose of possibility
Perfume all the world with your compassion
Wash away the mongers of the lie

Mongers of the lie
Deceptive 'til they die
They wear the mask of holiness
To and from the bank
It's you they've got to thank

Bon dea to my neighbours it's a new day
Lighting up the world with opportunity
To build a better world, how can I help you
To wash away the mongers of the lie

Mongers of the lie
Deceptive 'til they die
They wear the mask of holiness
To and from the bank
It's you they've got to thank

Good evening everybody, did you see the sunset?
The moon is on the rise before your eyes
Look above and share the love of moonbeams
Wash away the mongers of the lie

Mongers of the lie
Deceptive 'til they die
They wear the mask of holiness
To and from the bank
It's you they've got to thank

Photos in the Mail

A man hands me a loon
He says I like the way you dress
As I sit cross-legged beside the envelope
Marked Special Deliv, Special Deliv

Special Deliv from beyond the beyond
From Dr. Goo, photos in the mail, photos in the mail

They take my breath away like G-force,
in a steep turn, photos in the mail, photos

Black and white images
Combining and twining
Romantic arms in the mirror
Celebrating truest of loves with photography, photography

They take my breath away like G-force,
in a steep turn, photos in the mail, photos

Another guy interrupts me,
Glendon College 1972, I paid you
I asked him "Did you get your money's worth?"
He said he did, he did
As I sit mesmerized by these photos, photos

They take my breath away like G-force,
in a steep turn, photos in the mail, photos

Purpose

Once upon a time a conversation
A man asked me my goal
Me thinketh he meant purpose
As opposed to scoring in hockey
To be useful seems the purpose
Like mummies suckling babies
Mummies they are so useful
Mummies, mummies, mummies

Mummies yes they are mammals
Yes they have big brains
Especially when they use them
Like tulips in the rain
They have two lips in the rain

To be useful that is the ticket
To be useful that is the purpose
And that would be my conversation
So now I will eat some broccoli
Broccoli, broccoli, broccoli

Same Old Song

Kisses are like signatures
Some are structured, some are messy

Same old song, same old song
Flesh-loving man, same old song

When I need your lips on mine
Plant them quick like geraniums
Like geraniums, same old song

Same old song, same old song
Flesh-loving man, same old song

Shoulders so soft, wrists so tender
Succulent nipples facing heaven

Same old song, same old song
Flesh-loving man, same old song

Alabaster, viscous pendula, hypnotize me
Like some zealous worshipper

Same old song, same old song
Flesh-loving man, same old song

Equatorial, darkened rain forest
Perfumes my beard for next day's sniffings

Same old song, same old song
Flesh-loving man, same old song

Sitting in the Basement

I'm just sittin' in the basement
Waiting for paint to dry
Sitting in solitude
Water pipes running the mood

So I turned on the TV
Sunday Christianity
Almost Face The Nation
Rex Humbard's preachin'
Begging for my money
In the name of Jesus

Ignorance is cancer
God is not the answer
He will take your pants sir

Rex says he's troubled
He says he really needs the dollars
The cost of production
Necessitates donations

If you don't send the dollars
You will not be prayed for because

Ignorance is cancer
God is not the answer
He will take your pants sir

Slow Down Joe

I don't know where I'm going
You know I want to get there soon
I don't know when I'm leaving
I think I'll play a country tune

She says slow down Joe

I guess I'll have a jam with the sunshine,
Strum a chord or three or five
I don't really think it matters,
It feels good to be alive

She says slow down Joe

I don't know why I'm restless
I never thought to think about it much
I don't know why I do what I do
I guess I have a magic touch

She says slow down Joe

Socialist

I don't go to too many parties,
I don't have too many friends
I don't like too many people,
I'm not the kind that pretends

I'm just not much of a socialist,
And that's where my story ends

One to one is where I choose to be,
Any more than that is really company
Then all you get is a crowd
Then all you get is LOUD

I'm just not much of a socialist,
And that's where my story ends

The best friend I ever had
Knows me well and makes me mad
Like a shadow follows me everywhere,
And faces me when I stare

I'm just not much of a socialist,
And that's where my story ends

Some Dumb Machine

Why can't we stop and learn from our folly?
And listen to hearts instead of our wallets

The conscience of people got lost in the wash
Like socks that got eaten by some dumb machine

It's hard to remember dreams that you lost
Pursuing some policy without a compass

The conscience of people got lost in the wash
Like socks that got eaten by some dumb machine

Whatever happened to hopes for the future?
The dreams of a planet that mothered us all

The conscience of people got lost in the wash
Like socks that got eaten by some dumb machine

Sometimes

Sometimes I feel fulfillment
Sometimes I feel resentment
Sometimes I feel pain
Sometimes I feel so sad sometimes

Sometimes I feel mischievous
Sometimes I feel so redic-dic-diculous
Sometimes I feel love and kisses
Sometimes I feel ah, ah, optimistic sometimes

Everybody knows
Everybody goes sometime
Everybody lies
Everybody dies sometime

Sometimes I feel frustration
Sometimes I feel impatient
Sometimes I feel undip
Sometimes I feel undiplomatic sometimes

Temporary Love

Why do we preoccupy our spirits with possessing things forever?
Why not share the wealth and worry less about how long it's going to enrich our bank accounts?
Forget the metre, give your give, without the strings
If only for an hour

Temporary love, it's not so bad
Temporary love, it's not so bad
The love you give, the love you get
It's so delicious even over just a coffee break

You may feel expendable if you calculate your worth with a calendar or calculator
There is no category on the market for temporary love

Temporary love, it's not so bad
Temporary love, it's not so bad

You can call me strict or quite obese
But call me never ever after eleven
Cause I need my rest, I need my strength
To wage my war, I mean protest, against liars

Temporary love, it's not so bad
Temporary love, it's not so bad

They Will Take Your Pants

They will take your shirt
They will take your pants
They will steal your money
If you give them a chance
I say let them dance

They will violate your mind
On the dotted line
And they will squeeze you dry
Until you die
And maybe after
There'll be laughter

They will take your advance
If you give them a chance
They will "oink oink oink" for more
Because I'm a whore
Ain't that horrible

I have recorded this song many times going back to the *Sophisto* album in 1975. This song is a response to having signed too many contracts without a lawyer.

This Is the Song

I wish that I could be removed from all this waste
Of consuming lives and time, it don't rhyme with my peace of mind

So this is the song, you can hum right along if you get the urge to hum
You don't have to hum in tune, you don't have to stay in time,
You don't have to listen to this song
If it bores your mind

I wish I could see optimism in somebody's crystal ball
But all good things take time, I keep reminding myself every day

So this is the song, you can hum right along if you get the urge to hum
You don't have to hum in tune, you don't have to stay in time,
You don't have to listen to this song
If it bores your mind

Threading the Needle

I'm living alone
Cooking alone
Re-learning to savour
Re-learning to treasure
Threading the needle
Facing the mirror
Re-learning existence
And the dawning of distance
From you

Sweet spirited angel
Your romance enhances
And sweetens your passion
And fires your instinct
For threading the needle
And facing the mirror
The dawning and distance
From you

Still painting those paintings, and singing those songs
Writing down rhyme
Doing the job
And threading the needle
And facing the mirror
My energy's burning
And I'm blue

The term "threading the needle" refers to riding my fast bike in between two cars and living. The song is another kind of threading the needle.

True Love

True love is a mingling of the spirits
True love is surrender of the heart
True love is a bond without the bondage
True love is eternal as the stars

True love is a sharing of the moment
True love is a giving without the taking
True love is a storm that bears no malice
True love is the plasma of the conscience

But you cannot buy it
You cannot sell it
You cannot cage it
Because it's free

True love is a worship of the virtues
True love is the sunlight that never burns
True love is religion at its deepest
True love is the welding of souls

But you cannot buy it
You cannot sell it
You cannot cage it
Because it's free

Alcoholics

Alcoholics
They make me sick
They make themselves sick

Like Dr. Jekyll and Mr. Hyde
They drink
And they hide

You're all a bunch of fuck-ups
Who can't take a drink
The truth it ain't couth
What do you think?

Alcoholics
They come in all sizes
The rich and the poor
But they got one thing in common
They got the allergy
They got the allergy

Alcoholics

It upsets me that I wrote this song because it sounds cruel and I am not a cruel person. Back in '64 I learned from performing in vomitoria (bars) that people drink and drink and drink. That reminded me of too many people in my life. Alcohol is probably the most dangerous drug I know.

Friendly Cookies

When I think about the past
I feel the pain
I shall explain
Having ventured
Having witnessed
The truth it's sad
All too clear

When I think about today
I fear for all the lambs
The greatest flock in history
It's all a mystery

So when it's time to tally up
As Charles Darwin wrote
Friendly cookies
Friendly cookies
May be our only hope

Bake us all some cookies from yesterday
When life was less a mess than present day
Friendly cookies, hot and chewy
Take me back, take me back to Love Me Tender

If I'm not thinking about sex or motorcycles I'm always thinking about food.

When I think about tomorrow
I think October
I love her so
I do, I do
Because things are bad
And times are short
And we need a recipe
For friendly cookies
Friendly cookies
They're so friendly

Bake us all some cookies from yesterday
When life was less a mess than present day
Friendly cookies, hot and chewy
Take me back, take me back to Love Me Tender

Have a Nice Death

The evidence is clear
Dog knows there's plenty to fear
The scientists they all confirm
There's nothing really more to learn

Because humans are stupid
They piss where they drink
They shit where they eat
And then they repeat
So, idle your engines
Idle your brains
Idle your consciences
And have a nice death

No God will save you
He's just an invention
Of men who would control you
It's called freedom prevention
Did I mention…

Humans are stupid
They piss where they drink
They shit where they eat
And then they repeat
So, idle your engines

The song says it all.

Idle your brains
Idle your consciences
And have a nice death

Then you can light up a ciggy
And fire up your hot rod
And dupe your family
And rape their future
Because...

Humans are stupid
They piss where they drink
They shit where they eat
And then they repeat
So, idle your engines
Idle your brains
Idle your consciences
And have a nice death

I Am a Fool

I am a fool
I am a fool
I am a fool
That is the rule

I get so blinded
By flesh and perfume
She says woe is me
I volunteer

I am a fool
I am a fool
I am a fool
That is the rule

Just like a rabbit
Dumb as a doorbell
And I got rung
And I got snared
Because

I am a fool
I am a fool
I am a fool
That is the rule

I face myself, especially when I am foolish. Maybe I can learn.

In my experience
I have weathered sickness
But none like hers
Please spare me please

She's so vindictive
She is a cash register
She frightens me
She frightens me
Because

I am a fool
I am a fool
I am a fool
That is the rule

And I am stupid
Got stung by Cupid

I am a fool
I am a fool
I am a fool
That is the rule

Women Are the Only Hope

It's no secret that the human race has run its race or damn near
In the name of progress, the name of security, the name of convenience

Man rapes Mother, man rapes his mother
And the Earth is Mother, there is no other mother
So if you ask me, women are the only hope
If there's any hope at all

So much dogma and deception and perversion

Man rapes Mother, man rapes his mother
And the Earth is Mother, there is no other mother
So if you ask me, women are the only hope
If there's any hope at all

I Think of You

I think of you
Every evening
Almost
I think of you
In the midnight hour
I think of you
When I wake up
I think of you
When I think of you
I do
It's true

Then I think of you in the mirror
I think of you brushing teeth
I think of you climbing your staircase
I think of you on all fours
I do
I think of you

Boo hoo
Boo hoo

I think of you in my nightmares
I think of you spewing your vitriol
And I think of you and your racist mother

As the shrink told me,
the road would be bumpy.
I can learn.

And I think of you and your cigarette butts
I do
It's true
Boo hoo
Boo hoo

I think of you as lemon pudding
I think of you in your sweaty flannel nightgown
I think of you feeding little Pious
Then I think of you and your secrecy
I do
It's true
Boo hoo
Boo hoo

I'm Gonna Die

I got a hole
In my tooth
I got a pain
In my abdomen
I got a cough
I'm gonna die
I'm gonna die

I got a thought
In this brain
Close to my conscience
She keeps me sane

Maybe I'm dyin'
Maybe I'm not
Maybe is really
All that I've got
Maybe I am,
Then maybe I'm not

Experience tells me
I'm gonna rot
Back to the ground
Maybe the ocean
Maybe the sky
I'm gonna die

Cremate me crispy.

Ya know Leonard Cohen
claims we've all known
we're all just bubblegum
Chewed by fascists
And lied to daily
Ain't no maybe
Ain't no maybe

Maybe I'm dyin'
Maybe I'm not
Maybe is really
All that I've got
Maybe I am,
Then maybe I'm not

Oxymoron

I'm an oxymoron
I love to contradict myself
I'm an oxymoron
And my finger's on the button
And my nose is on the razor
And my tongue is fairly certain
So you move,
move to this groove

I'm an oxymoron
I'm the king of humility
Threading needles religiously
And I'm navigating imagery
And I'm navigating injury
And tolerating wheels that spin
And the answers are not in books

Give me an 'o'
Give me an 'x'
Give me a 'y'
Give me a moron
Because I'm an oxymoron
Yes I'm an oxymoron

I'm a narcissist.

Scientist

I am a big old baby
Almost forty-four
I am honest
I am single
And I will not bore you

I've been wrong
I've been right
I've been heavy
I've been light

I am gentle
And aggressive
And I'm on a mission

So you can call me
a scientist
Doin' research
I am a scientist

I am E.T.'s mother
I am Jesus Christ's conscience
I'm a prophet
I'm a porker
I'm a cockroach on a good day

I consider myself a man of science. I trust my eyes, my ears, my nose and my toes.

What do I require
A woman generous of spirit
A woman active and focused
A woman scientific
So you can call me
a scientist

I'm allergic to cigarettes
I'm allergic to felines
I'm allergic to hypocrites
Even to myself
So you can call me a scientist

Shepherd's Pie

You are the shepherd's pie
of my eye
Aye, aye

You are the broccoli
The one for me
Me, me
You are my honeybun
The only one
Yum, yum

You are the borscht I love
with sour cream
Cream, cream

You are the shepherd's pie
of my eye
Aye, aye

I equate food and love
as one.

Deemo Crassy

Stephen Harper, he's a world-class hypocrite
He's a world-class meanie, he's a world-class weenie
Stephen Harper, he has no vision
He has no empathy and he hates your children
And he hates democracy, I'm speaking
Deemo Crassy

Stephen Harper, he thinks he's sharper
Because he can govern by photo-op
And obfuscation, he'll try that prorogation
Just to change the station because he hates democracy

Deemo Crassy
Deemo Crassy
Deemo Crassy

I say call a doctor, call Duff Conacher
Please call Ed Finn, Maude Barlow, Pam Palmater, Judy Rebick, Karen Robinson

Deemo Crassy
Deemo Crassy
Deemo Crassy

Acknowledgements

My thanks to Gwen Swick for her savvy critique. And, more thanks to Karen Sue Robinson (Mrs. Joe) for typing up the produce.